Body and Echo

Jennifer Burd

Plain View Press
P. O. 42255
Austin, TX 78704

plainviewpress.net
sb@plainviewpress.net
512-441-2452

Copyright Jennifer Burd, 2010. All rights reserved.
ISBN: 978-1-935514-53-4
Library of Congress Number: 2010923423

Cover art and art on pages 5, 33 and 65 by Charlotte Hodes.
Cover design by Susan Bright.

Acknowledgments

Poems in this collection that first appeared in other publications: "Neck X-Ray," *Southern Poetry Review* (University of North Carolina, Charlotte; Winter 1994);"Patience," *Nobody's Orphan Child* (anthology by Red Sky Poetry Theater, Seattle, Washington, 1996); "Seeing, Believing," *Into the Teeth of the Wind* (University of California, Santa Barbara; Volume II, Issue 4, 2002);"As if a Flower," "The Red Geraniums," *Eclipse 2004* (Siena Heights University, Adrian, Michigan); "Chronic Illness," "Loving Paper" *Eclipse 2005* (Siena Heights University); "Field of Vision," *Eclipse 2006* (Siena Heights University); "Hunger Addresses Her in Midlife," "Work In Progress," "Luna/Because," *Bridges: A Jewish Feminist Journal* (Indiana University, fall 2007, issue 12.2); "Hunger, At the Soup Kitchen" and prose versions of "Luna/Because," "Conversation Piece," "Work-in-Progress," "Shaman," "Encounter," "Sunday Dinner," "Silas," "Loretta," and "Words" appear in *Daily Bread: A Portrait of Homeless Men & Women of Lenawee County, Michigan* (Huron, Ohio: Bottom Dog Press, Inc., 2009)

I would like to thank Charlie Burks, Simone Yehuda, Claudia Schmidt, Nikki Louis, Phil Tobin, Christina Morales Hemenway, Donna Gotlib, Lucia Saks, and Marie Thompson for their encouragement and close readings of many of the poems in this book.

Thanks also go to Larry Smith, publisher of Bottom Dog Press, Inc., for permission to reprint material from *Daily Bread*.

And special thanks to Dick Fortune, for the inspiration and support.

Contents

I   5

As If a Flower	7
Hunger Addresses Her in Midlife	8
The Warning, The Crossing	10
Chronic Illness	13
Impact	15
The Window	16
Neck X-Ray	19
Seeing, Believing	20
Field of Vision	21
The Red Geraniums	22
Two Views	23
Upon Finding an Old Family Photograph	24
In Summer	25
Walking Home at Dusk	27
Forecast	28
Off Season	29
Chicken or Egg	30
Aubade	31
Cut Sunflower	32

II   33

At the Airport	35
Wonderful Time, Wish You Were Here	37
Chicago Windows	38
Letting a Train Into Your Life	39
Lumber Mill Ghost Town	41
At the Art Museum	43
At the Aquarium	45
In Winter	46
Dancing on the First Evening of Spring	48
Patience	50
Detail	51
Vespers	54
Procession	56
Meditation: Tracks in Snow	58

Solstice Hymn	59
Infinity	60
Voice	62
Reading Constellations	63

III   65

Loving Paper	67
The Fire	69
Reporter	70
Luna/Because	72
Conversation Piece	74
Work-In-Progress	76
Shaman	78
Encounter	80
Sunday Dinner	81
Silas	82
Loretta	84
Words	86
Hunger, at the Soup Kitchen	88
Vertigo Chicago	91
Domestic Scene	92
Cleaning Woman	93
Possession	94
My Life As a Lake	96
Homage to Trees in Late Summer	98
About the Author	101

I

As If a Flower

Now I wonder
if somewhere a young
girl is tasting
the first pleasures

of starving her body, *no*
dawning inside her
as will exceeds
the rooted flesh.

As if a flower
had decided to weed
the petals from around
its open face

or a cloud chose
only cirrus – distant,
crystalline, unable
to thicken and rain.

Or the river itself
gulped back,
leaving the banks
intact, reaching

now tentatively
to the sea, having swallowed
its own torrent

Hunger Addresses Her in Midlife

Remember, I invented you –
separated you from the stars,

gave myself to you
selflessly
so you would survive.

But then you turned
on me, refused
the seeds I laid at your feet.

Now you have gone back to the beginning
to learn the original lesson again.

It will be harder this time.
Like the gray squirrel digging
hole after hole in the front yard

as the snow melts –
you have forgotten where you have hidden
your many desires.

Believe me, when I urged
sublimate, darling, I was giving
you the only advice you would accept.
And didn't it send up exotic,
colorful gardens after all?
In the most unexpected places, no less?

But you are much older now,
you have fallen back
on clichés to guide you –

If you need me
you know where to find me:
I slip into your tight black dress.

The Warning, The Crossing

She looks to be about 14,
the French girl – her face flickering
across the aisle
as her native tongue skips stones
upon the river of her speech –
sun and trees licking
at her, tricking her in
and out of all the ages of her life
(each flickering a stroke, a mirror:
her face/my face).
All at once the shadows of alders
cast her into full woman-
then freckle childhood across
her nose – *en train* – it's all spelled out
in light, that place where one's whole life
is worded in time-of-day.

I recognize the unsigned contract
that light has placed
on the empty seat beside her
as she takes her chances with back turned
to the moving window, (*was/is*)
where the wounded glow of late afternoon
merges *before* and *after*
at thirty-frames-per-second and sun and shade
flick us in and out of present time
like night lightning

○

Waking into daydream, middle-age,
I strobe to the window of the last car, the rails
in the forefront gleaming into vanishing –
and back. She is pointing
her American companions' attention
to the distant mountainside. *Comment est-ce qu'on dit?*
(How does one say it in any language? How,
in the language of light?) *Water-fall?*
She puts her mouth to the sound
and drinks. I taste its source (*was*) –
last hope from despair (*is*) –

untranslated. She looks up
and I am covered in graffiti, the text
of her hands indistinguishable
from the light and dark flashing
across my body. The shadows gain an edge
as day gives way, slowly widening
their own banks in search of contact,
the fluttering minutes bringing me here
having somehow brought me here
by way of sun-sliced-and-shadow-repaired
memory not yet memory (the shadows
themselves a torrent, sunlight hitting only the tops
of the trees) until now:

adolescent flaring-into-warning
like a swimmer gasping for air;
the trail of her speech leading me on,
deepening overtaking the whirling branches,
bending them to its will.

Continued

Moving ever closer to Evening, we skim
the miles of labor beneath our wheels
(so many loves lost),
now past the station at that small
and experienced town, now past
the warning and the crossing (*was/is*),
the *oh well*, the *forever*,
and the familiar foreign voice
talking faster, sharper, softer –
the slim arms gesturing excitedly
in the near-dark, indistinguishable
from the mature limbs, endlessly repeating
like the signal up ahead,
like the single gesture to come

Chronic Illness

It's like this: as if
a singing, secret self
had been packed away in the attic
for the longest season of the year. As if
those garments were no longer
needed – too much, or not enough,
depending on the season.

And it being set apart, you begin to forget
what the weave of health
feels like against your skin –
the way the face of one
who might have been a lover
is obscured by time,
yet still nags the heart.

And so it is in this you must
trust: what you are being shown
through absence. Not like the aftermath
of thunderstorm, in which the emptiness
itself is form. *This* lack drizzles in,
until you do not realize
it has colored everything. Instead,

its quiet drama simply becomes
tiresome. It changes your life,
but, finally, not in colorful ways.
Still, you must learn to love
it unconditionally, like the relative
who's overstayed her welcome.

Continued

○

They say the body knows
its way to health the way
sea turtle hatchlings know
the luckless path to surf
and go halfway around the world
without being shown.

And what a reunion it will be then –
you'll open the trunk lid,
delight in the things you hadn't thought about
through all that weather,
and bury your face in them.

Impact

Perhaps a startled dove
flew overhead and we heard,
above afternoon traffic,
the sound of feathers
brushing by and so
became momentarily freed
from the panic of sirens,
shouts, theft, perhaps
it was our natural calling

a longing to fly
bleeding out of the blue,
hit-and-run. The sun blinked
and we folded like night petals.
And then the sky breaking
overhead, like a wave, as we came to –
that color suddenly become
intractable with our lives
piled against it, with no
birds to distinguish it
from pure metal

The Window

Late afternoon
       far away
from the scene of
   the accident
a lilac bush has been
           growing
a long time.
    Lavender translates
       into patterns of bright
and dark
   onto the floor

      of my convalescence

as the remedy
      carries me
           out of myself
and the window
   teaches me all   I need to know
of stasis inside a larger
      whirling –

In midlife
      no immediate
  family
neither here
     nor there

backward
  nor forward –

     The window drifts
  in and out of
          my half-sleep
suddenly seeming   to be the reason

for small boys
   in baseball caps
           trailed
by a Black Lab
on a red leash –

     adolescent
   girls coming home

from school on time   the sun
   lighting their complicated
       faces
as a bicyclist

feels the tug of road
   and a spider spins
       against the heat –

And thought
is a curtain drifting
      in and out
          of an open window

  wafting with any
available breeze

dappling the room
     with sun and lilac
  which marry
just this side
     of the pane   dancing
past a chair

Continued

    where light
          glances
                    breaking

    into twin colors
        of glass   of air
     around the hundred-year-old
        photograph of nobody

    remembered

        the early-summer afternoon
    reassembled
      and transfixed
              by its own heaviness

    in the facets of the crystal doorknob

Neck X-Ray

Stepping stones
leading to the planet

of my head.
A string of butterflies

poised for the flight
of my next move.

Preserved in a moment
as dark as *far*,

a wondrous stellar
curve, spine to brain,

linking me to my eyes:
ancient ancestors

facing a night sky;
their fear of never

being meant to see
themselves so literally –

Seeing, Believing

> *Henry Ford collected Thomas Edison's last breath in a glass vial,*
> *to be put on display in the Ford Museum.*
> *(Stated in an NPR report, January, 1999).*

How he must have waited
with baited breath
for the final invention
of the man's lungs –

the idea filling itself
to luminous proportions
in his hands:
beyond the lensed eye,

housed in a display case in
his namesake museum,
something
solid as science,

visible as belief,
falling and rising
as the night guard nods,
under its own private light –

Field of Vision

Skagit Valley Tulip Festival, Skagit Valley, Washington, Easter weekend

There is some kind of religion here.
In this countryside where the river *Skagit*
has risen repeatedly to make the valley
one piece, and old barns have been brought
to their knees, we pilgrimage to vast tulip fields:
This is a red to fall for
and rise up again, a waking wider
than your maker ever provided. Strangers
arriving from all over, bloodrelatives,
hearts making for sky, the most
lavish sight the eye could own –
your body lying open there

The Red Geraniums

Red geraniums
distract the eye, while up high,
the wind arranges
and rearranges tree branches.

Just on the other side
of the fence, where sight can't quite go,
a lark lies on the grass, buried under
lightly tossed handfuls of shadow.

Two Views

On an early spring evening,
the hill of houses puts
its great navy overcoat on,
buttoning it closed
with the three red rows
of blinking lights on the summit's
twin radio towers.

The shy usher, middle-aged
and scurrying to and fro between
bright venues at the foot
of the hill, can be seen turning
toward a wall each time
she gets into her dark
coat, buttoning

Upon Finding an Old Family Photograph

The image fades into a light
leak on the upper right –
what some believe
death looks like.

Around my young great-grandmother
Susan and her leg-o-muttoned sleeve,
the plank of my great-grandfather's
arm – he looks protective,
though his strong hand is barely
visible on the overexposed white
of Susan's right shoulder.

My grandmother is a girl
playing outside the frame
or perhaps indoors.

And I am somewhere
in this picture – even in black
and white I recognize
the hydrangea-blue shade
from another life,
the old people's gardens.

Circling the tidy structure
in the background (part of the house?
A barn?) my eye tries the door,
noticing how it is pulled
tight – how it is shuttered
for years, the latch rusting flat
against the decaying slats,
eventually turning *me*
into a door, so often
will I have begun
to imagine the other side.

In Summer

Toward solstice, the days upraveling
and there is waiting
in every reach of the tree (the wind
stirring the leaves, the hint),
and the mottled shadows on the roof below –
calm as a cow's hide.

The notes of the church bells
have nothing to cling to, nothing
to penetrate, really, just the continuing
and what it contains – the broad day
going nowhere (the built-in ache) – and the river,
the one-sided conversation.

Nothing hidden under flat sunshine –
it's too easy, all that knowable,
each thing following the other,
and I mirror that pedestrian growth:
winter's winter! What *within*

am I looking for? What *deep*
is in the evening sky
that I can see but never touch?

Where is it I want the leaves to take me?
Why can't I undo myself
in the spaces between the leaves?

Where in the bark,
where in the roots (the tree
denying its mysteries), where
in the uncomplicated moon?
Where in the passable?

Continued

But I've always wanted time
to stand still, and it is tall
in the hot summer afternoon.

Yet it's always just answer, answer, always
hello, always, *yes, let's do something
or nothing, it doesn't matter,*
the days giving themselves away

like salesmen's leaflets, making us feel
desirable, yes, but not really asking
anything of us, the understanding
requiring no wound.

Walking Home at Dusk

Fireflies trail like sparks
from a still-smoldering day.
The crescent moon harvests clouds
while corn falls quiet under evening mists.
Crickets have one thing to say: *this, this.*

Forecast

Against the fence by the spent
hydrangea, the casual talk of two
bright blue and white folding chairs
overheard beneath the red sky at morn,
the beheaded sunflower stalks.

Off Season

Lake Michigan, mid-September

The groom is black and white,
and the bride in flowing gown
and veil white as the gulls
hovering like mothers
seems to take no notice
of the swarming black flies
that keep us in the water,
remote. Nor does her long-
sleeved mate brush them
from her bare arms
as she trots in the vacant sand
fluffing her train. But with three
marriages between the two of us,
what advice could we give?
Certainly not to be practical
and swat. Or, *Come on
in, the water's fine*. They smile
at an image of themselves, framed,
as the photographer keeps
backing away from them,
taking aim, the cliffs eroding
in the distance, the soft waves
foaming along the shore.

Chicken or Egg

From Chagall's "Bridal Pair at the Eiffel Tower," 1938

Blue is where losses accrue
like dowry. All the tokens
are in place, the tower divides before
from after, and the bride has just taken her face
off into her fan. She is turned toward us, away

from the blessings of violins, animals, angels, *him*,
and the safe heat of candles
while the idea of the perfect union
floats above and they glow
in its yellow egg-light.

So that she doesn't see she has just wed
the mature bird, though she leans
into its piles of dirty clothing
and scuffed children almost visible
beyond the green smoke of summer foliage

while behind her, the marriage site
is already uncontained, in flame –

Aubade

I have left my old life and years
of solitariness behind.
I have moved so many times.
This time it's with you
I'm loving that vague bewilderment
of waking in a new home
like suddenly noticing
the change of season.

Let go, the cracked teacup,
a missing vase,
the old cost-of-doing-business
as pictures, books, and furniture
find places for themselves
with room to spare.
Through a cool window

the sun rises noticeably
later, but the afternoon will grow
hot nonetheless. We realized last night
the fireflies are gone –
they may have been absent for days.

A goldfinch clings to the single
sunflower, which studies the ground
in the dewed and drying garden.
A new scent steeps in the air.

Cut Sunflower

Morning inside my kitchen
all day long. A walk

at noon in a hot Dakota field,
endless sky

leading me on.
Evening in my lover's garden,

a lamp shining out of dusk.
Muscular stem and leaves –

promise of days and more days....
Overnight, bright pollen

dropped on the page.
Above, an older woman

gathering up her golden skirts,
full of seeds.

II

At the Airport

It's being able to rub elbows
with the planet's travelers, yes, and hear
the rosy milieu of foreign voices,

but also being utterly filled with place,
destination, even though we are just sitting,
standing, trotting, as we did

in the old hunter-gatherer way.
This is the communal hearth
where we act out stories of the world –

Big Myths –

and the tale ending with us
climbing into the belly of a giant bird
and flying away.

But for now, feet still self-assured,
we ooze transience like a secret we can't keep,
are here but not *present*

(we have permission, everything now liminal) –
pulling bags packed with essentials,
talking our own ears off.

All these millenia later, how we still delight
in telling and retelling this one, letting fly
our collective joy, terror, love.

It is written all over us
even before the wistful captain
makes the decision to engage

Continued

the landing gear of what has now
officially become
our connecting flight

Wonderful Time, Wish You Were Here

The black overcoat
abandoned by its peers
who'd gone off in twos and threes
to bars, hotel rooms, and streetlights
hung out alone in the Grand Lobby
all night. It saw whole galaxies
wheel across the polished toes
of bellhops, night blooms glow
beneath vast skylights, rendezvous
coalesce and disperse without any
actor, agent, or witness to cast a shadow.

It heard all the Musak turned off.
It saw elevators open and close their doors
for the pure joy of emptiness.
What it took for an understanding
of the name-tagged night clerks
was quite possibly just the white wings
of butterflies forced from pupae
and released, brushing its collar
in shafts of moonlight –

Chicago Windows

This city of windows!
Some call this
progress.

Eyehold by eyehold
our gaze advances
into sky.

Along the elevated track,
other windows move
horizontally into the future,

One face
lit
in each.

Letting a Train Into Your Life

And it doesn't tell you when
it is coming until it crosses midnight
at neuron and synapse....

And you think you couldn't possibly
have enough space to unpack
an entire freight schedule

along with all your old clothes,
the chipped mugs, and the throw rugs
you lay down here like track.

But you make room for it
in unexpected places – between settings
at the dinner table, between a book

and its word, the ear, the heard –
and each time the grinning rail
whips that harp between those slick lips

you give it permission to
whistle through the drainpipe,
stoplight, night flight –

hum in your ear, shiver
your spine, be your time –
sing between the sheets, roll in

its compulsion for order
its music that leaves you
in such a state

Continued

rumble its numbers
down the sheep-counted vertebrae
of your sleep, allow the walls wheels

until the honeymoon is over
and you simply turn
toward its 3 a.m. caress, in sleepy bliss….

Lumber Mill Ghost Town

On November 30, 1995, the Port Gamble, Washington, sawmill, the oldest continuously operating sawmill in the United States, closed permanently.

Far from midwestern roots
and the first generations
of northern European farmers
planted there, I could feel
the Old Country
in this now museum of a town
built above a real
fire-breathing dragon –
the sawmill alive
since 1853. There were, as well,
a few mid-century homes
full of quaint, silent things
with no dust on them,

a postmaster
with empty hands –
ear to a radio
inside the otherwise vacant
mailroom – and a cemetery
crowded as a saloon,
brimming with immigrants.
I floated among them
while the sun shone brightly
on the stones like birthright.

Downhill, the old dragon
was being put to bed.
I could almost hear, above the shouts
of workers and sighs of machinery,
the first managers' wives
talking on porches, new

Continued

accents hewn in the street,
children playing on the green.
And faintly, the anxious
rending of paper –
envelopes carrying news
to Germany, Scotland, and Sweden.

At the Art Museum

Gazing into the vanishing
point along the ox-trodden

paths of certain
500-year-old paintings

time and place framed
by wood and metal

the gallery vault
decades of your own

longing
as you are defined

by the white space
of the walls and the silence

gathering around you
and from over the shoulder

of the young art student
circling Breughel with her thoughts

moving on to a moment
photographed above the wet

streets of 1930s Paris
to enormous undulating sculptures

touched on every surface
by the entire universe

then climbing to the second floor
and disappearing

Continued

behind the backs
of the bored gallery attendants

into the mountains
of the old Chinese scrolls

At the Aquarium

The whole day was the night
a splendid old lady
emptied her jewelry box onto her hands
and fanned
gold-bronze-gold
and silver self-reflecting light
before she swam away

In Winter

Just when I only want it
to be over with,

I am edged into being
by what the tree knows

about spring but won't say,
night's deepest thoughts

as day. For one who loves
morning, there's a place to live

in those clear recesses
of south, where it's sunrise

all afternoon
until a sky with no need

to cling to anything
hangs a star

and the moon reads
the meaning out loud,

falling through the branches.
Just when I wonder why

I must belong to a land
under hard freeze,

the mourning dove's silence
above the snow calls trees

out of the blue
so I can see the pure

shape of the world,
each day born

unadorned, stripping me bare,
promising everything.

Dancing on the First Evening of Spring

March 20, 2007, 8:07 p.m.
For D. F.

Another dance on another cold night.
But at the stroke of equinox
our gaze locked
and held me there
for what could have been an entire season.

   I couldn't know then
   how, later, the weightless hours
   would vanish like early spring snow
   as I'd fumble for sleep until

   the sound of frantic wings
   would draw my hazy doze
   to a sparrow pair
   coupling against my window.

   Or that the next dawn,
   sleep elusive still,
   I'd find a few twigs
   gathered on the outer sill.
   Or how, after decades

   weaving through our separate lives,
   these young months – now grown, flown,
   returned – would keep knitting longing
   into our body-lengths of skin
   awakened by spring thunder,
   a drenching rain.

Then the music took off
and we flew,
turned, held fast, and parted –
engaged a final time,
thanked each other

and went our separate ways
into the crowd of dancers
seeking new partners.

Patience

Like the good gift,
it can be found
in small places:
between the hot hours
of a summer afternoon,
between the hand
and the motion of repetition,
in the flecks of silence
between distraction.
It is a tiny nation

that can still be found
on the map, though its name
and inhabitants have changed
since the war. Inured
to our hurry, the old-country
ancestors simply roll over,
breathe a sigh through the grass
and into the trees that says
My, how the time flies.

Detail

For Nellie Maude Bender, 1875 –1965

The trees curry favor
in the evening, in summer.
The light is old, very old,
the strokes that things are painted in –
   stipple light

frothing in our minds: a small branch
and leaf lit as if secretly
to nourish just one part –

shadow, the significant other
(how a bird flies underfoot):

a moment tempted
out of time, the specificity
yet lack of commitment,
surface heightened and then
indistinguishable from context –

so we leap from moment to moment
of each other, flamelike, our irregular
patterns of feeling rising
and receding, catching –

          O

My great-grandmother's *Lilacs*, 1897,
lay against the wall
near a corner of the room,

Continued

darkening. And a look falls
across the fainting couch beneath it –
the inside of the old people's houses,
Michigan rooms in childhood.
I remember her

frail length on the couch
enclosed by the indoor dark
of a summer afternoon,
a tea darkness, staining,
containing hidden signs: her words
were always *Where did you
come from?* – and the years between us
obscuring her question
against my reply: *San Luis Obispo*
was where I was born.
I felt age that monumental
could not have meant anything

less literal. Yet, I couldn't tell
from the text on her face, just what she thought
of what I said. Then I would run
back out into broad daylight.
Old age wasn't where I lived.
I had to get big before I realized
she meant something

more local, something closer
to *Lilacs* and the play of light
and dark over and around
the blossoms and leaves, the white spray
shining out of the indoor shade,
blooming from the canvas in May
of another century, the floral scents
pouring through an open window –

light and shadow cast
by windy hardwoods ringing pattern
across the floor – the blowsy
concentration gathering around her hands,
her eyes. One hundred miles from home
(having already studied the light
in paintings much older and farther away)

she gave play to her dapplings,
painting the shadowed depths
that would recede into the green decades,
the young art student poised with her brush,
waiting for me to grow into her –
automobile, airplane, moonshot...

the years of becoming
now falling between us like summer tree shade,
the shadow-bridges I skipped over
from one windy continent to another across the yard,
the way I paint *Lilacs* with her now:

the *blue-purple* of the dark sprays,
the *dark* and *darker* of the rich leaves,
the weave of the basket against the brown
background, the white that won't fade –

light now become my hand
upon the page. Light – the small bones
of the hand, porous, ringing
and ringing the trees –

Vespers

Haehnle Preserve, Jackson County, Michigan, October 2007

We were all arriving to praise
sunset in our way –
75 assorted humans, eyes trained
on the wetland, the thousands
of sandhill cranes due in
for their evening roost,
and the headliner: the one
stray Whooper among them.

Born in Wisconsin, bound
for Florida, his trackers said the bird
veered, lost his "internal compass."
But among all of us – heir to ages
of innovation and desire – how many
had toggled east to west
before landing precisely *here?*
What tangled threads
had our own flights woven?

Spotting scopes, binoculars poised,
waiting, waiting in the chill
dimming light and polite chat
with others united by feathers
and hollow bones,
waiting

and suddenly in my secular
mind's eye, fresh in
from some childhood tundra,
a line of birdwatching nuns
in pale habits soft-landing,
lilting down the hillside
with their vision out front of them,
magnified, the whisper of their steps
a pure call

to mauve and fuchsia coming down
and more waiting,
then the first purring sandhills gliding in
by twos and threes, legs trailing
with the delicacy of grace,
and at long last, the exotic

enormous white wingspan
jaunty and true as devotion,
releasing us into a collective sigh
issued like prayer,
and soft applause rising up –
startled rock doves
on a city street corner –
and the flock of women
dissolving into evening mists.

Procession

On a day in this season
of vacancies (the bare trees

holding them aloft
in their arms, the snow

sounding them out
to the ground), a line

of whitened mourners
is leaving the cemetery,

having circled this small
city of stones – not

like seekers or sightseers,
not like commuters

but in the soft-treaded
way of animals

in their native habitat,
having slipped past

a pair of hooded lions
guarding the children's path

to the neighboring woods –
vehicles now exiting

slowly, single file,
as if not to disturb

what nature must do,
each carrying a small

piece of absence
away into the early dusk.

Meditation: Tracks in Snow

How we withhold our surprise
at these hollows, the traces

of our coming and going –
how confused and so vulnerable,

the small boats
made by our boot-soles,

frayed around the edges
amid the frozen whitecaps.

Our tracks stand alone
yet are inseparable

from the body's pendulum,
what awaits our arrival –

even now as we turn to look
at this late evidence

trailing behind us.
Born orphaned and hopeful,

being the helpless separation
between what has been, will be,

from which an entire life arises –
each points simply to a future,

the imprint fully present and grieving
the memory of its birthweight.

Solstice Hymn

Northfield Church Cemetery,
Northfield Township, Michigan

A page of writing
on either side of a country road:
A field of stalk. A field of stone.

And the good plain fields
receiving the snow.
And the sunlit snow

receiving the wind-blown words
of the few birds
that haven't left for winter.

And the rows of folk
beneath the good, plain words,
the sunlit snow that stalks the stone,

the few birds left
to write the winter fields,
turn the page –

Infinity

We keep trying, but we just can't
wrap our minds around it:

night grown large
in the uncountable rooms of a tree,
rivers in winter,
stones.

Everywhere but nowhere so large
as a clear dark sky –

silver spoon of our universe, dotted
with destinations.

○

Tucked between strangers
at the planetarium, I look up
at Bear, Hunter, a cluster of sisters
rescuing us

from that lovely free-fall blink
when we dare think
no end in sight.

When the lights come on
we stumble out
into a second, larger night

with a real moon shining down, pointer
to the body's fear:

You are Here.

○

I locate constellations
on my "Junior Star Finder,"
chart my course
for North, Jan. 15, 10 a.m.,

and constellations wheel invisibly
through the blue-day sky:
Pleiades. Ursa major. Orion.

A cluster of five river stones
rearrange themselves mysteriously
across my tablecloth
and I lose myself in the dark

of one skipping-stone flecked with white
encircled by a white ring –
a map of stars called down
from the rooms of trees
to help a snow-bound river find the sea?

○

Looking out
we call starshine bombarding us
from 150,000 light years of dark

a place, a design
where the eye can light
that won't keep still...

Voice

Remember the trees'
long shadows are meant
for you. See how tenderly
they touch. See how they stretch

your future out at dawn, then fold it up
and tuck it away, safe, at noon
when you are at work, lunch,
the market, then roll out

your childhood each evening
until the very dark
you were once afraid of
comes to claim it.

○

Long ago, you stood
under leaves in the rain.
When the sun came out and lay
all the shadows back down

at your feet, you hopped from one
blowsy continent to another
across the wind-swept lawn.
Then one day, the light

changed ever so slightly.
Do you remember
how you turned toward brightness
like flowers in the garden?

It was no longer the leaves
but the spaces between them
that sheltered you.

Reading Constellations

> *All truths wait in all things – they neither hasten their own delivery nor resist it.*
> — Walt Whitman

Light walks morning-clean
through the window
without saying anything.
I open my hands
to make an offering

or a sign of surrender –
leaving it up to light
to know which.

◯

Every line in my open palms
leads to whatever it is
I need to know. Together
they make a map

and I spend the day
wrapping and unwrapping objects
with the most local geography,

making momentary gifts
of just the right thing
at the right time.

Continued

○

With every fleck of my body
borrowed from the universe,
I grow large
each time day and night converge –

matching the sunset to the silhouette
of childhood's ancient tree
rooted inside me.

○

As light is my witness –
the making, the going.

○

Holding my hands up
against the pinholed dark,
I don't trust myself
to find my way by the constellations
they frame and yet
I trust the way –

○

Late at night, when all things are given
back, the maps lie unfolded,
a vacant landscape – imprint
of the stars beyond the roof.

III

Loving Paper

is the sure sign
of a writer, my mother
always said. Which must be
why the straight, invisible cuts
hurt more than certain larger wounds.

As a child I didn't understand
what she meant by "growing pains"
(though I tried to feel them as the tied
feet of some Chinese girls I'd heard of),
unaware that their signatures

would come through my own freehand.
Meanwhile I learned how the original page
became ruled, punched, bound.
Later, paper was a shield, the journals
keeping womanhood at bay

for years, years that don't easily talk
back, though I address each page
like a mother, rereading the boxes
of adolescence that delivered
growth's necessary deformity,
the drafts of adulthood

written all the way into my body:
two authentic starvations, ump-
teen cycles of binge and purge,
the hunger that finally settled
for the paper and words. So that now

Continued

I show up at paper's edge
each day, hoping to feel my weight
between the lines or in
the heft of hand to pen to page,
hard labor.

○

Somehow it hurts, remembering
my first experience of loving
paper, how I saved my entire
nine-years-old allowance for every size
and shape of notebook I could afford
to admire: how I ruffled

the leaves, nosing them over
for scent. How I caressed
what they might hold, marking
years before letting ink touch them.
How the utterly empty page
was still beautiful then.

The Fire

How I still need
to keep it with me,

how I use it to make
my way through the day:

hunger like perpetual morning,
trellis for the vine,

giving resistance, weight.
And like the sun

I rise raw, ravenous,
keeping the ancestors close by –

so many labors to get here. At night
you can see their lamps

along the river, glimmers
of hope. There on the far shore,

they are shaping their blades
while technology advances

and Hunger keeps watch....
I, too, need those edges

to hone myself on,
to wrap the bone around me.

Reporter

I am here to record
their words about hunger.
I will horde them
in my slim reporter's pad –

designed to capture the essence,
efficiently, discreetly.
They chatter like birds
about the weather

inside the cozy soup kitchen,
where their need doesn't label them
failure, but *regular*.
I want to know

how hunger led them here,
what kind of map it has made
of their lives. And what kind of future lies
beyond the sweet peas in butter,

soup bowls, and chicken pot pie?
I am answered by
the *tsk* of the fork
to the plate, the whisper

of the biscuits to the gravy.
the gossip of the gingham curtains
to the plastic centerpieces.
Can't you see it's cold outside?

What I don't tell them
is that hunger brought me here, too.
That I once sheltered
emptiness

as a way to feel
my outlines against the world.
Teenager refusing
to let my body be forged,

there was a time
I would have felt myself
splintering
under the mercy

of this very meal
that makes them one body –
the soft dough,
the warm gravy.

I ask them how it feels,
court objectivity.
The volunteer servers
always offer me a plate,

no questions asked,
and every time
I politely refuse.
Instead, I write.

Luna/Because

Luna says the problem is darkness,
that it's her disability –
I have to be home by 8.

Because 15 years ago just like yesterday,
the rapist broke into her house while she slept
and started punching my lights out.

And even though she needs you
to hold her at the soup kitchen,
touch is a traitor

and now night is a place
where the razor blade tricks her
into its slick caresses

because *men always
seem to want something* and *they never
mean what they say.* Because

she wants to show you her scars:
a galaxy of stars up and down her arms.
Last week she got a new

permanent. *To feel like a woman –*
but she thinks her dark
hair makes her look depressed

and today she has a coupon
to make herself blonde.
She's grateful for the Dollar Tree,

so she can buy something
to make herself feel pretty.
Is that too much to ask? She asks anyway,

because the disability check
only goes so far.
Night keeps coming back.

Conversation Piece

I catch up with Jim
in his wheelchair, pulling himself
along the street with his feet.
He hears the voices of angels
when he sleeps, and worries that the pain,
or the cure for the pain,
is making him *insane. Nothing stays*, he says.
As soon as you write the word "bird,"
it flies off the doggone page.
I've only just met Jim,
and I don't know what has happened to him,
but I like the way his words take wing.

Jim and I go way back,
according to him. Back before the soup kitchen,
even before time, *when your mountain fell*
next to mine. Today he says we have
a daughter, and that to save her
we'll have to empty out the river –
empty it of restlessness, religion,
Faith, Hope, Charity. And that we have to
come up with something on which to agree
or disagree by 1:30.

I tell him we can take this conversation
and decide what to name it.
He rolls a cigarette:
Well, they've already beat you
into the mold, but I'm glad
I didn't see it. He says we have to go down
to the river bank and stand there,
with our feet in the mud. Just
stand there: *And would you come along*
in a little white ball? And where
would our daughter be then?

Now I've lost track
of how many conversations
we've had and where they all were,
but they stick with me – the traces
of our long-lost girl, places,
the people we might have been.

Work-In-Progress

Daily Bread of Lenawee Soup Kitchen, Adrian, Michigan

Each week like magic, a mural
blooms a little farther along a wall

inside the soup kitchen.
Each week – where outlines

of those kneeling by a river,
addressing a hungry crowd

or holding up empty bowls
have been waiting for color

to fill them, show them how
to work, teach, weep, hope.

There are crosses, men in long robes
and hands raised toward the sky.

Skin-and-bone farmers plant seeds
in dry earth and an old woman

pushes a shopping cart past a man
asleep in a Dumpster. It's a story

of bread and water and distances.
It is a human scene,

repeated in the lives
moving through the soup kitchen

each day between noon and 2.
There is already a signature

in one corner,
but we never see the artist.

Shaman

I walk over to his table
at the soup kitchen
and Jim tells me I'm doing
some pretty good sword handling

then he asks me
if I've heard from the daughter
he says we have
living in Arizona.

I don't tell him I've stayed
childless by choice
all these years. Don't tell him
there have been times

I've wished for a child.
I say that, no,
there's been no word,
had he heard anything?

His face clouds with concern
that she and I may have fallen out
and I explain that part of the problem
is that I can't remember her name –

I wonder if he remembers.
I don't know sweetie, he says.
*All I know is when we leave
someplace as a shaman,*

the box leaves with us.
We look at the mural
on the soup kitchen wall,
a story of hunger and salvation,

and I ask him if our daughter
is in the scene. He points to a small,
dark-haired figure in a red dress.
I ask again if he knows her name.

Stephanie, he replies, then turns
and asks if it's *rough* on me
not to be able to see her, and do I
portray that hurt in everyday life?

Then he points to the woman
in white, standing in a river:
*That's you. Because her hair
catches fire but never burns.*

Encounter

Sitting at the soup kitchen
lunch counter, I sipped
coffee while Kevin
downed a hot meal.

He asked if I'd heard
he'd been mugged.
I told him I had,
but that I wanted to hear

the story from him.
He told me how
the mugger took his Social
Security card, a brand-new

calling card someone
had given him, his last four
dollars. How he feels the guy
put a gun to his back

while he's crossing
a downtown parking lot.
And when Kevin tells him
he's homeless, the guy says,

Give me everything

you've got, then runs away
into the dark after taking
the gloves bunched up like fists
in Kevin's jacket pockets.

Sunday Dinner

I sit down next to Patty
at one of the soup kitchen's
gingham-covered tables.
There's never any wait:
plates of food appear instantly.
I don't know Patty well,
but she talks nonstop
about her past, cutting
her ham into tiny pieces
and giving me the months
her first husband took from her –
beatings, burns from cigarettes,
darkness in a locked closet.
But it was only their son
who was *really* taken from her,
she says, when he was put
into foster care. She pauses
to give her knife and fork a rest,
allowing a smile to claim her face.

Soon, she says, she will see
her son for the first time
in 25 years. *I get him
for Mother's Day,* she says.
Father's Day, too.

Silas

Even with a full plate,
he doesn't stop talking
as he sits inside the soup kitchen,
his brand of cigarettes – "Boundary" –
peeking from the top
of his plaid shirt pocket.

It's nearly 2 p.m.,
and soon the kitchen will close.
He tells me how he's out of work
and somewhere between high
and low. How, years ago,
he was vice-president
of a local company before
depression disappeared him,
and does so again every now and then.

The kitchen will close in 10 minutes
and we'll have to go.
But his food grows cold
as he describes the dangerous business
of cutting trees for cash,
the ripoffs, lost equipment, injuries,
and his plans to build on the property
he owns where he lives in a shed.
How he has 13 different medications
and a team of community health professionals
to keep him from opening up
his wrists again. How he wants the story
of brain chemistry told.

With just a few minutes more,
I wonder if he'll get
to the square of chocolate cake
a volunteer set beside his plate
half an hour before. On the frosting,
a section of a construction scene –
part of a bulldozer, and an orange diamond
that says "Road Work Ahead."

Loretta

She's a writer, too.
This time, a novel – by hand
and sometimes with a typewriter.

She doesn't want to give
the plot away but says
it's not about her life – not

about quitting
her childhood at age 9
to take care of her mother

not about leaving high school
while Mom got better
then moved her out

not about her first marriage
her disabled son
or her second husband

who lost his job
when the car broke down
not

about barely getting by
on government benefits
the soup kitchen and

so little time. Her soft voice hides
the distances she must walk
to get things done today.

Her long brown hair follows
the path of least resistance,
falling on her shoulders and back.

She gets ideas for writing
by going out and walking around –
seeing people, she says.

*Sometimes I go down
to the tracks – that's good for it.
The tracks talk to me.*

Words

For David Hamilton, 1957 – 2004

I

From the back of the room
at the funeral home,
it looks like you except for the hair
that's too-combed down. It seems strange
to see you there, no longer
even needing the shelter
of a body. Your ex-wife tells me
that if I look in, I'll see you
with a copy of The Daily Telegram.
I remember how you used to complain
that you couldn't get groceries
or underwear on your walks
between the bridge you slept under
and the library downtown, where you stopped
almost every day to read the paper.

II

Saying he knows you can't speak
for yourself, the minister puts words
in your mouth: "If David were here,
he'd tell you to use his passing
as a wake-up call for getting
closer to God."

Thinking about it later,
I remember you as a man
who used his own words.

III

At the memorial service
we each are given a small square
of paper and a pencil
to write down something we want
to say to you. They are private thoughts
we don't speak or claim you with.
Later, the words deliver themselves
by leaving their forms
as, one by one, the papers
are burned in a fire over snow
by your open grave.

Hunger, at the Soup Kitchen

Middle-aged and wiry,
wearing faded blue jeans,
he's already sitting
at the lunch counter
when they pour in.

They ask him if it's any good
today. He just nods
and sips his black coffee,

endless refills of black coffee
and lets others do most
of the talking –
Ya hear the weather report?
Whose birthday is it?

Hunger has known them
all their lives and they are
his regulars. He loves
them, loves even

their hangovers
their body odors
their broken homes.

He calls them
one by one, sends them up
for the day's special:

Now everyone wearing green, now
mismatched plaids, now everyone
whose name starts
with the letter S. Everyone
with an aching heart –
it's chili time.

He is bad news.
He is good news.
And news travels fast,
even among those with no
phone, car, or mailing address.

He is the fly
on the soup kitchen wall
above a mural where urban
hunter-gatherers forage
in alleyways and starved farmers
beg for mercy, rain.

Hunger has no place
for shame, no patience
for the flirtations
of mere *appetite*.

See how he helps this one
make up her mind.
See how he helps that one
pick a fight. He fawns over

their disheveled hair,
nicotine-stained fingers
and charity clothes. He fetches
extra napkins, more ketchup,
eavesdrops on every conversation.
When they think he's not

listening, they make plans
never to need him again. But he
just finds their hope charming,
knowing nothing ever begins
until he says so.

Continued

Now Hunger watches them grow calm
as the soup kitchen nears closing,
makes his move
when he senses they are full:
Let me roll that cigarette for you.

He is proud to have taught them
to leave even before they are asked to –
only the first of many more choices.

As he holds the door open,
the last one shuffles out and squints
into stark sunshine with its small shadows,
the streets and sidewalks scattering
in all directions.

Vertigo Chicago

The Blues leak from a pool
of innocent bystanders
surrounding the one-man
band, shoot up

the gilt and straight-faced sky-
scraper. Inside, the wrists
of the ones who've made it
insist on interesting lunchtime.

Back at eye level, the street
vendors are just making it.
They feed their clientele
without even looking up,

knowing hunger regularly
comes down to them
inside the revolving shadows
of the big and timely money.

Domestic Scene

They're at it
again. Everyday words
rise from the driveway, break
from the background hum, bleed
through my misted pane.
I strain to hear, attracted
like violence to the wholesome glass
between us – how the young wife
once again brings him up to speed,
puts him down, leads him
to justify then abandon himself.

The little girl realizes
her privileged position.
For a mere instant her body
stiffens and her eyes start
as she begins to sing
and dance around her mother's
legs, as if to strengthen
the contrast between their bodies
that daily diminishes.

Cleaning Woman

The sun rises round
and bright as a new coin
as her muscles begin to knead
themselves toward the shapes
of clean houses. For a moment
she feels small and light;
but the summer scents don't take
her far. She is intimate
with the surfaces at hand.

She glows for the kitchen floors,
sighs over the living rooms,
puts her hair up
for the master bedrooms,
wears gloves to handle the baths.
Fatigue, the relief, steps in

to dispose of the remains:
hair, nail, and skin; paper scrap,
cracked toy, dirty ribbon, cup lip;
even the copper coins
she's swept from dusty corners,
picked out of the laundry
basket, mined from the davenport –
knowing they've been handed
importantly to small children
whose awe was brief.

Possession

My keys lay tumbled
on the table, each a keeper
of secret and fact

nesting naturally
awkwardly together
like the pink and beige shells

my fingers find
so desirable so far
from their addresses –

shells I collected one day
along the shore I wanted
to lose my way home to

because like the hermit
crab I can't stop
moving on

○

Riddle, puzzle piece,
spoiled brainchild –
one key is

not a destination,
not even an address.
It is not here on business –

indifferent
to the matter it opens and closes,
the opening and the closing

and the worlds on either side
introduced
never discreetly.

It is just a key –
piece of jagged metal
tool with one trick

tool fashioned with other tools
into the idea
of a door to lock behind me

key with no hunger no
possessions just a readiness
for the one true home

My Life As a Lake

> *On the eastern shore of Lake Michigan*

I'd almost forgotten,
before emerging through the trees,
the blue expanse inside me –

stretching out beyond eye's reach
yet lapping at my very feet.

Horizon, my father.
Shoreline, my mother.
And the water that is present
in every dream.

In this one I am
a foot soldier,
collapsing in the shallows
of my past.

In another, I welcome
a stream into my life.
In still others, I swim skillfully,
if anxiously, with the Big Fish

or fall to my knees
in surf, dazzled by the light
spelling my shape.

Some say that so much water
in dreams is a sexual gesture, the deepest
need to create. But what about the waking
dream – the one about *order, order?*

As if it's too much
responsibility to be the water
in this dream. Water,

coming into contact
with everything on earth –
so omniscient, meaning also
helplessly local. There must be danger
in so much inundation and surrender,
in so much lonely undertaking.

But isn't it the same,
this wringing forth
of meaning from the page?
How is it possible to bridge

the twin desires
for paper's clean edges
and what takes place
on the expanse they contain –
desire equally for limits, certainty,
and for transformation, possibility?

Meaning, to live always
in this discomfort: knowing
it is the water in my nature that keeps
the steady illusion
of shoreline, of horizon. Water,
my very own hero:

I know I am inseparable
from what is setting sail.
And the city on the far shore
I feel but cannot see.

Homage to Trees in Late Summer

Solace begins
in the green-dark spaces,
(no beginning, no end,
no need to contain) –
recesses
promising mercy,
no need to choose
between shelter and stars.

All whispers start here, *leaf mercy*.
All rumors of before and after:
indefinable
places between
and
(looking all ways at once)
branch mercy
above
the too-early gold
curled brown underfoot.

All wounds start here: bark mercy.

All saying starts here: wind mercy.

All healing starts here: rain mercy.

Gather under
look up and read
(*by the flame of deepest*
root mercy)

the messenger mercies
bird, dew, and sun,
that have brought us.

It is the time of year:
the plump drop
into a relaxed hand,
fruit given you who would take
these uncontainable spaces
for beginning and end.

Again: no need
to choose between shelter and stars.

About the Author

Jennifer Burd has lived and worked in many parts of the United States and currently resides in Ann Arbor, Michigan. Her professional employment has included work as an editor, instructional designer, writing instructor, and journalist. Burd received her BA in English and her MFA in Creative Writing from the University of Washington. She has had poetry published in numerous journals and in the anthology *Nobody's Orphan Child*. She is also the author of a book of creative nonfiction, *Daily Bread: A Portrait of Homeless Men & Women of Lenawee County, Michigan* (Bottom Dog Press, Inc., 2009, with photographs by Lad Strayer), based on her experiences reporting on local homelessness for the Adrian, Michigan, *Daily Telegram* newspaper. Burd currently works as an editor and writer for HighScope Educational Research Foundation in Ypsilanti, Michigan.

www.ingramcontent.com/pod-product-compliance
Lightning Source LLC
Chambersburg PA
CBHW052107070526
44584CB00017B/2372